To my grandma in Heaven, this is for you. Thank you for being my guardian angel and keeping me safe. I love you and miss you daily.

A special thanks to Mrs. Sandy Murray, who saw my potential in writing before I knew myself and to Mr. Spencer Stein, who introduced me to new writing techniques. The influence of you both has inspired me to keep writing daily. Thank you, again!

I. The Movie "Notebook"

    I always wanted a love so deep, so deep that there would be the possibility of drowning. I don't know if that sounds dark, and maybe it is. I want to drown in a love that I can't escape. To fall so deep in the cracks and the bends and tares of your heart, to be supplied with what only the heart can give. I want to feel the beating of another heart other than my own. I'll tell the rain to come and those storms to carry on because I want to see your darkness for what it is and love you unconditionally. Show me the parts that others didn't love about you and I will love every last one. For love, it isn't running when you see someone's flaws. Our flaws make us insecure, but I'll love your flaws, then love the rest of you too.

    I want the everlasting, the never ending, and the infinity. Forever just isn't long enough. I want to hold your hand and feel the nerves connecting. Beyond depths of horizons, I'll see your eyes in a million sunsets. And so be that those eyes of yours are baby blues, golden browns, pasture greens, or galaxy grays, I would never look away even if my eyes became blinded by loves first sight. If it ever meant climbing through the gates of steel to reach your love, I would. I need to know, that if the earth froze over, your love could burn fire into my soul and bring me back to life. The type of love that sneaks in, enlightens the soul, and brazes the skin. I don't want to look up and have prince charming there, I want to get lost and be found.

    You, love, have the power to trigger happiness within myself, the world needs you, I need you. A crowd full of faces, but yours will be the only one I see. May the best moments of my life, be the ones spent smiling while gazing at your face. Just to spend more time with you, I'd count every strand of hair on your head. To keep you in my memory I'd look in your eyes every minute of every day. I'd outline every inch of your jaw and neck with the tip of my nose to smell what love designed for me. And with my lips, kiss every part of yours with a slow exhale of breath. Your flowers will bloom because I'll be the water to your roots that grow so deep.

My heart, until conjoined with yours, isn't a heart at all, you see. In my book, you will be every chapter and every reader shall know my love for you. I can't promise many things, but I can promise that you will be loved, and be loved so wholeheartedly. I want the type of love, that, when I grab the keys and say let's go...right by my side you'll be. We'll drive for miles, having no clue where we are going but knowing exactly where we are, with each other. I want to look at you and say it was always you, it will always be you. I can't say that I'll be your sun when the rain won't stop falling, only because the sun still shines when the rain continues to fall. Instead, I will be your umbrella; no sadness from tears should ever touch you.

The minute I see you suffering, my heart will suffer too. If I could, I would take every ounce of pain away. Although an ounce is just an ounce, it's still pain. When the alarm goes off in the morning and we both get ready for work, I will enjoy those precious moments as the sun is barely shining through the window. When that ray of sunlight hits your face, I will then be reminded why I love waking up in the mornings. At the end of the day, when the sun is going down and the weight of the day's workload is finally off our shoulders, I will run into your arms and place my hand on your face... the only thing I have wanted to touch all day. I will look at your hands while running my fingertips across them, to feel the all the hard work you have done, just so I can live happily.

I will cherish you as long as I live. I could lose everything, but better yet, I'd give it all away if it meant keeping you. The universe is big but it would be small without our love. Looking forward to every second of every minute. The butterflies don't disappear; they continue to grow and grow each day. Soft flutters when our eyes meet, and a calm serene when you attach to me. There is something about when two souls come together. It's unexplainable, but what it understood should not have to be explained. Two bodies like sparks when ignited by touch. One and one, balancing each other out. Neither the depths of the ocean nor the height of the sun could measure the amount of love between us two. The pink sunset in the sky, the rainbow after the rain, nor the deep blue color of the sea, could amount to how beautiful our love would be.

      When I say I'll never leave, I mean that. This thing called love, between you and I, will keep me with you forever, because I know I will be afraid to lose you. You will be my happy ever after, my happy beginning. My life will change forever. If the whole world turned their back just know I got yours covered. If we ever must be apart, just know I'll carry your heart with me wherever I go. And when I can't sleep at night, because the absence of your arms, I'll look up at the moon and feel your warmth; I will feel your presence. There is something magical about the moonlight; it can change the mood of anyone with its radiance. For me it will make missing you easier. Wherever you are right now in this world, just know I am ready. Ready for it all. I will speak of you and if the universe so happens to hear, you will find me.

II. My Blessing My Curse

Being a good person has always been my blessing
and my curse.
Having a kind heart hurts.
You feel the most pain, yet you give the most love.
You get cut and stitch yourself back up again,
just to go back loving the person that cut you.
Always looking out for others,
when they never looked out for you.
You don't notice your pain
because you are worried about theirs.
It doesn't matter if you're happy- if they aren't
there is no point.
Making promises,
walking barefoot across the world
for something they would love.
Staying up late at night
listening to their fears.
Traveling far and wide
to make sure they are okay.
The sacrifices,
people with good hearts make.
Even if someone
shows little to no interest in you,
you still find yourself attached to them
because you see the person in them
that they don't see themselves.
Reaching out both hands
to lift them up.
There are so many people out there
who destroy the innocence of kind souls like mine.
They feed on the authenticity of innocence.
To say I am empathetic
would be an understatement,
but there are no other words
to describe what it feels like
to feel the pain of the person

sitting next to you.
It's hard.
I sat by my friend that day,
when she cried about the death of her brother.
I sat by my friend that day
when she looked at her sleeping child
as she was crying,
asking what she ever did
to deserve such a blessing.
Each time,
their pain was my pain... and
I had never felt anything so intense.
Those were the first times I knew I could carry the pain of others.
I couldn't explain
why some days I woke up
with a heavy chest
until I figured out my gift.
I build people up,
I demolish their insecurities;
I am their light in the darkness... but
I haven't found my light.
I sit in darkness too sometimes.
My kindness is my blessing,
my kindness is my curse.
I don't think people care for me
as much as I do for them.
Not everyone will understand me,
not everyone will care.
Loving too much
keeps you awake at 3:00 in the morning
wishing you didn't have feelings at all.
Loving too much
keeps you up at 3:00 in the morning
thanking God for feeling so much.

III.   The Repairable

I know a lot of people who are broken by life and maybe you are one of them. But remember, what's broken can always be fixed and there is no such thing as... impossible. Step outside the box, do something different, change your scenery. Don't go looking for greener grass, make YOUR grass greener. Wake up before dawn and smile, for those around you are asleep and peaceful but the sun has awoken and the birds have started flying. Happiness is all around you, just change your perception. Sit on the rooftop, and look at the stars. Listen to your favorite song and play it on repeat. Don't stop going until you are satisfied, but even then, keep going. Be so content with yourself, that if someone asked you, "If you could be anyone, who would you be?" I hope that you would always choose yourself.

You see, a butterfly cannot see just how beautiful its wings are but the rest of the world can. You may not see how great you are, but I do, we do. They admire its beauty just like others do to you. Make peace with your past, things happen for a reason. Never compare one's life to your own. We all carry crosses but we all see sunshine too. Find all the perfect things in your life, forget the rest. Fall asleep at night with a heart that is so full of happiness, you can't wait to wake up the next day. Give this world a chance to show you that there isn't evil in every mile. There are so many reasons to go on living happily. Fix what broke you and then continue living.

IV.   My Wedding Day

As I watched my best friend dance with her father that day of her wedding, so many emotions filled my head and my eyes. I tried to hide the tears but there was no forcing them back. All I could think about was my future wedding day. I won't have my father to walk me down the aisle nor dance with me on the dance floor. I want that so much.

I believe that everything happens for a reason, but I am not sure what this reason is. Why I am the girl without a father to love me. It is very unfortunate because I love with so much of myself and one of the most important bonds any girl should have is with her father, and I missed out on that my whole life.

It was heavy on my mind, but I knew I wanted someone to take my fathers place so I asked my brother. He said he would gratefully do it. Although it won't be the same, I know my brother would do the best he could to make sure I was a happy bride on the day of my wedding, even if that meant filling in for my father. After all, my brother has never left and he was the first boy I knew to love. Forever by my side he would be. That alone will make my wedding more special and unique. I also made the decision to have my grandpa step in for the father daughter dance. He may even join my brother in walking me down the aisle.

It's not about who should be there, it's about who was there and who will always be there and I know deep down in my heart my brother wouldn't miss this for anything. Along with my brother, I'll have my sister there right beside me as my maid of honor. I don't know what I would do without my little sister. She says she is the only person that can be mean to me. Anyone else?? They will catch her wrath. But that's it... that's what family is for. I'll have 2 of the most important people there that day along with other family and friends and because of that, I'm more blessed than I could ever imagine.

V. For you, the one who hurt me

If I could go back and do it all over again, I wouldn't. And as crazy as it this may sound, thank you for hurting me. Because you hurt me, I know that one day I will find the one man who will change everything and I will know what real love feels like. You have opened doors for me, doors to another man's heart. To another heart that is more than willing to give love. Even though you were the reason why my chest hurt, my heart broke, and my soul cried, I still wished you the best. I wanted to hate you, I wanted to despise you, but my God did not form those feelings into me. All I could do was care for you still. I wanted to understand why you hurt me, but what I wanted to understand more was why I still cared for you, why I still talked to God about you, why I still sent Sunday blessings to you, and why I still prayed for your happiness. I wanted to understand those things but God said that was beyond my understanding and that praying for you was the highest of all callings. Praying for those who have hurt you is the best thing you can do. Life isn't about giving to those who are worthy, it's about giving to everyone. Life isn't about what you gain or what you can receive, it's about what you give.

I feel like I didn't get my chance. You only saw a glimpse of what I was made of. You said you didn't think you would ever find happiness, but funny thing is, you seemed happy when I was by your side. Was it all for show? Was I some fling to boost your ego? Or were you pretending?

I went above and beyond, and I stretched myself thin. Only thing is, I was happy to do that for you. But I didn't get the same treatment. After things fell through with us, I wondered why there were people like me. Why we would stretch ourselves thin for someone who wouldn't even do the same for us in return? I remember you promising me the world, and then you walked away with it. You left me broken and torn.

I wanted to take every problem you had going on and help you fix them, but I see now that those are problems you needed to fix yourself... They are inner issues that I can't touch. If you can't fix yourself for me, how am I supposed to help?

I wanted you to challenge me with my goals and aspirations, but instead you and I challenged each other, like 2 boxers in the ring. Fighting. You would push and I would pull, and I was the one on the ground in the end.

Life had already dealt its fair share of challenges in my path, and you added to the chaos instead of helping me conquer them all. Until you heal yourself, you will only be a deadly weapon that kills a girl's heart.

I wanted to give you a chance to redeem yourself. I offered a second chance, because we are all human and we all make mistakes. I didn't think in the back of my head that you would blow this, because I thought by then you would have realized just what you had. Some of us mean our words, others just say them because they sound good; I think that was you. But unlike you, I meant it when I said you were important; I meant it when I said I'd always be there. Crazy thing is, I still mean those words, even if you don't feel the same.

My heart is big, but space is limited. Yet, I made room for you. Now that space is in total chaos. I'm trying to clean it up but you left such a mess. I don't know how long it will take me to repair this room. If I let someone else in, there might not be space for a next time.

I can't blame you or tell you that you are wrong because that wouldn't be right of me. I don't know what goes on through your head 24/7 and I wish that you would have let me in. I wanted to understand the things that you were going through. Maybe a relationship is exactly what you wanted, to be taken seriously, to be happy... but you didn't know how. And that is okay. Maybe you were scared, because something so real was right in front of you. I don't know but it doesn't matter anymore. My heart wanted to care for you, in good and bad, to protect you, even on the days I felt weak myself.

However, through all of this, I learned that my heart may shatter but it won't turn black and cold. It beats harder, and loves more. I genuinely hope that you make it where you want to in life and that the rest of your days be filled with happiness. I just hope, one day when you think of me, you know that I was the girl that was always there, the girl that would have always been there. I want you to know that I would have done anything for you, and you let me go and what you don't know is that there is someone out there for me, already on his way.

VI.   Dark Garden

Somewhere between having hope and feeling hopeless, the garden grew dark flowers,
And along with the rain, the clouds brought despair and tainted showers.
Once upon a time, the petals were bright, and full of life,
But their stems were severed with the piercing sharp knife.
The leaves began to hide and their surface doors shut,
But no one knows how they continued to grow, despite being cut.

VII.   My Story, Your Story

Each of us has a story. Our stories differentiate us from everyone else in our lives. My story might make someone cry; your story might make someone laugh. But regardless of the genre of our stories, we each just want to be heard, whether we want to admit that or not. The thing about me is, I don't want you to tell me your story. Let me find out. Let me look into your eyes and put the puzzle pieces together.

VIII.   The Girl God Blessed

God knew what he was doing when he created me. One ingredient at a time, he added the sweet, he added the kind, and he added the humble. I always hear how sweet I am, how good of a person I am, and just how humble I am. I can thank God for that. I get told that I am an angel in human form. I can also thank God for that. I'd be lying if I said God didn't bless me with a big heart. I believe it is something you are born with. At the end of the day, my heart usually hurts more than the normal heart should, but that's the thing, I don't have a normal heart but I always feel like it's been worth it.

I forgive easy, just as if I had never been hurt before. I have wanted to hate those who have hurt me, but my God did not add those ingredients. I found that out when I wanted to hate them but I didn't know how. My heart tends to take over my mind a lot. I can say I have never been stuck between what my mind tells me to do and what my heart tell me to do because my heart wins every time. I used to ask God why I was a chosen one to receive such a big heart but I stopped asking questions because he's God and he makes no mistakes. I love my gift from God but it hurts me sometimes. People walk out, stop talking to me, hurt me, take advantage, lie, and even try to damage my heart but instead of revenge they just get added to my prayer list.

I am a girl who loves God! Because of him, I am fearless, and I am stronger. I am bold, yet quiet. My faith shines through my spirit. But I am not perfect.

I still have moments when I feel undeserving of what God gave to me, I still sin, and even though I trust in my God, I still feel empty and alone. He knows. I admit that I have put things or people before God and I have asked for forgiveness. I am a normal person, just like anyone else; I just keep loving, keep praying, and keep believing. My faith leads me to believe that even in pain you can find the positive. I lean on my God. I yearn for his love. I know that I am not perfect but he believes in me so much that I try everyday to make him proud of his creation.

This big heart of mine has been called vulnerable but I do not see vulnerability as weakness. God started with a plan, and I will continue with his purpose. How I love God is how I love others. Because I love my God, I need my relationship to honor him. A relationship without God in the center isn't a relationship at all. I will challenge you to see the world differently. My heart from God has lead me to see that life is beautiful in many ways I never thought possible.

I love more deeply, more fully.

IX.   Not Different. Just Me.

I am not like other girls, and that's a line you have probably heard from every girl before. You are probably wondering if it's true just because so many told you the same thing. I have been through my fair share of failed experiences. I have given love to those who weren't deserving of it. I realized that, having me is like winning the lottery and why would anyone wait to cash in their winning ticket? Well there were some guys out there who didn't believe that I was their jackpot. Regardless, I have remained the same winning ticket; I just haven't fallen in the right hands. Maybe the guys before feared commitment but I was taught to never run from my fears. That's why I invite commitment in with open arms.

I am genuine. I care not only for you, but your well being. If you're down, I'm down with you. The only thing is, we aren't going to stay down because I am going to lift you up. I will always look out for your well being, I will always make sure you are okay, and I will always be your star.

I am sweet. See the thing about me is, you will never see me angry. I could have the worst day ever, but when I see you I want you to be happy so I will bring nothing but positive vibes your way.

I am not selfish. You will always be my priority. There are too many selfish people in this world who only care about themselves. I am not one of them. If you find yourself needing me, I will drop what I am doing and be there by your side.

I love. If you ever feel like you need love please come to me, I have plenty to give.

I care. I don't ever want to see you sad. Your feelings mean more to me than you could ever imagine.

X.   What I'd Do For You

If any man treats me like a queen, he deserves the world and I will give it to him. I want him to be happy with himself, his life, and his experiences. I want him to succeed with his goals and aspirations. Most girls want a man that's already put together and well established and as there is nothing wrong with that, please don't knock the ones who still have growing to do. I know that am not perfect and have a lot of growing to do myself.

XI.   Your Lost Pieces

So you lost all the pieces to your heart, let me help you find them. I understand that you can't hold all of them and put yourself back together again, so that's where I come in. Let me hold all the pieces and one by one I will hand them to you. You must learn how to heal yourself, but not forgetting you have me by your side.

So the pieces aren't sticking all the way, let me be your glue. If you have them in the right spot, I'll be the bind that holds them all together until they become stuck.

You probably feel unworthy right now, with your heart shattered and exposed in front of my eyes. I would too. But please don't feel that way. I will love you, broken or not. My eyes not only see the beauty on the outside but on the inside too. Yes you may be broken, but right now you are completely open and I can see right in. My idea of beauty has changed, now that I can see your soul.

For you are not what others see in you, you are what you see in others. Promise me you won't forget that you are loved.

You know, I have tried not wearing my heart on my sleeve, but, to be honest, it didn't feel right any other place. Because of that, my heart is scratched and torn. One day when it's time for me to put the broken pieces of my heart together, I hope you will be there to hold my pieces for me.

I know that right now, mentally, you are probably exhausted from the past relationships that hurt you and it's not your fault at all. I will love all those insecurities. I know what it's like to be shut down because someone didn't accept your flaws.

You keep telling me it's not as easy as I am making it sound but I don't give up easy and I never stop trying. I know that I too am a work in progress and far from perfect.

I have been broken so many times; I feel like I've lost some pieces along the way but please believe that I won't let you lose your pieces.

And that dark side you keep entering, I am not afraid of it, because, as you can see, the darkness is my territory but there is always light in the dark.

XII.   God's My Point Of View

      I am someone who has wanted to be married and have kids before taking into consideration what God wanted for me. Now, I'm not saying I don't love God and that I don't want nor need Him, I'm simply saying I spend most of my time noticing that everyone seems to be married and having children but me. When has God never been enough for me? No, I am not okay with being single but I shouldn't wallow in self pity because I'm not. I have God by my side and with Him I should be happy enough. I should be so happy and so content with the life I have now that "looking" for my future husband shouldn't be my number one priority. When that day comes, I will be overwhelmed with joy, sure, but until then, I will remain praising God, who on a daily brings me blessings beyond measure.

      I ask that God help me put my focus back on Him. If I seek God first, He will put the right people in my path. I don't want to lose my focus on Him. Through it all, God will remain the center of everything I do. That's the way to live, that's the way to be. God is making me wait, so I know great things are coming. I believe when God makes us wait; we should be prepared to receive more than we asked for.

      Many people these days are in relationships that God never approved of; I want God to approve mine. Before I commit to anyone else, I need to pray about it and make sure he is the one God sent to me. If you think about it, there is no rushing God's timing. Love will never compromise my walk with God. I don't want Him to ever think that I doubted Him or His timing. If I wait, it will truly show God that I trust Him and I trust His plans for me!

      I know that if I take care of my relationship with God He will take care of everything else that is going on in my life.

The best relationship is when you can praise God together.

XIII.   A Piece From Imagination

You showed me how to fish, how to reel it in when I felt the yanks from my pole; you showed me what a genuine smile is.

That's the smile I had when I caught my first fish. You kissed me and told me how proud you were and right then and there I knew I loved you.

You showed me how to play your favorite video game, the difference between the buttons x and y; you showed me what it felt like to be hugged warmly.

That's the hug you gave me when I heard my first "mission accomplished" from the game; you told me how great I did for my first time. I knew then and there I'd never stop loving you.

You showed me your little pond behind your house and how to skip rocks on the top of the water; you told me to watch the little ripples as they blended out and together. You said it was the most beautiful view until you saw me. You showed me just how special I was.

That same feeling I felt after I finally skipped a rock after my one hundredth try; you picked me up and swung me in a circle, like I had accomplished something big.

You introduced me to God. I always heard the name, but to be honest, I didn't know much about him. No one ever took the time to teach me. As we sat together in Church, your hand placed on mine, you taught me how to pray.

I remember the words exactly, "Dear God, thank you for another day and thank you for this un-promised day. Thank you for everything you have done for me and everything you will do for me in the future. Place your protecting hands over my family, the love of my life, and I. I thank you for the girl right next to me; I know you made her just for me and I can't seem to tell you thank you enough. Help me to love her and treat her like the princess you created her to be. She has changed my life God, now I want to change hers. If it is your will, God, help us both grow closer to you in prayer and in love. AMEN".

    I had never said a prayer before either, but his was the most beautiful thing I had ever heard. He kissed me on my cheek and we enjoyed the rest of Church hand in hand. I never missed another Sunday again and every night, I prayed to God, "Dear God, thank you for another day and thank you for this un-promised day you gave to me. Thank you for bringing someone so special into my life, who introduced me to you. My life has forever changed. I want you and I want him forever by my side. Thank you for watching out for me and saving my life."

    And every night after my first time at Church, I knew you were the man I'd love for the rest of my life.

XIV. For The New Year

I expect 2018 to be different but it can only start with me. Every other New Year I would fall short of my dreams, goals, and aspirations. I let the negativity cut me 2 weeks into the New Year and I had officially told myself that this is how the rest of my year is going to be. Not this year, 2018 is going to be different and I can feel it. My goals have even changed. Of course, I want a better lifestyle like going to the gym more, but my goals go deeper than that.

I want to love myself. I am 24 years old and I can shamefully say I don't truly love myself. I found this out in 2017 because I found myself altering my dreams and my goals for guys who "let me" do that. Instead of pushing me to follow my dreams, I found myself following them. I let them convince me that my goals could wait, or that I already exceeded well beyond my means. Mistake. No woman should ever settle for where she is now because she knows there is more out there for her. No woman should ever tell herself "this is good enough" or "I'll be fine for now". We have so much living to do still and settling is just a roadblock. I didn't let them love me for who I truly was and that's how I knew. Any girl who loves herself will push towards her dreams and when obstacles stand in front of her, she will knock them down.

I hid certain parts of myself from people. It was like peeling off the shy layer or the impatient layer and hiding them under a rock. If I pretended they weren't there, no one would walk away from me because of my flaws. In 2018, you love me or you leave me, and that includes everything. If I can learn to love the parts of me that go unseen, the rest of the world may grow to love them too.

I'd be lying if I said I take risks. I don't and that needs to change. I am a big comfort zone person, but I know deep down inside I am missing out on the world and all it has to offer. I used to set goals, but always fell short of achieving them. This year, I'm setting them, chasing them, and achieving them.

      I want to love, not just romantically, but really love. I want to accept people for who they are. I want to explore new mindsets and environments. I want to gain deep connections with people and feel nothing but pure happiness when conjoined with someone. I see so many lonely people wherever I go and I was one myself, but this New Year I am going to change all of that. I want to build relationships with new people but I do not say new people freely. I mean new people that challenge me, that excite me, that love me, and understand me.

      I want to feel happiness. I spent 2017 looking in the wrong places, searching where I had no business, and confiding in people who ran me off the tracks of happiness. I want to be able to lie in bed at night and feel nothing but peace within. I want to look forward to waking up in the mornings. I want to spend 2018 helping others find their happiness as well, to encourage, to uplift, and to inspire. I want to be so happy that even when I am confronted with a trial I will pull myself up and know that this is a bad situation, not a bad year.

      I know not everyday is going to be perfect, and there will be days when the whirlwinds are just a little stronger than tomorrow's, but I will teach myself the beauty in disaster for I've been told that perceptions shape reality.

XV.   Something I Wonder

Sometimes I wonder if I wake you up in your sleep. Do you wake up reaching for me; do you wake up calling my name? When you wake up and realize that I'm not there, just know that it wasn't my choice to leave.

Do you ever dream of me, and wish that things could return how they used to be? Do you ever wake up at 4am with thoughts of me and tell yourself to go back to sleep?

Our love story got cut short; it ended too fast. I was convinced this was the last relationship I'd be in but how quickly things changed.

You stopped reaching for my hands as often, you stopped touching my face in the mornings, and your lips started to feel cold instead of warm. All these things happened without warning.

I remained holding on. Not noticing that by holding on, I was inflicting more pain on myself than I would by letting go. I held on to our ropes so tight that blisters, scrapes, cuts, and redness started to appear on my hands and palms.

Suddenly it's you waking me out of my sleep. I am the one reaching out for you in the middle of the night; I wake up calling your name. And when I wake up and realize that you're not there, I know it's because I wasn't good enough anymore.

I am the one dreaming of you, and wishing things could return how they used to be. I wake up at 4am almost everyday with thoughts of you, telling myself to go back to sleep.

XVI.   First Time Eye Contact

They were green, so deep and so dark. The sun came by and his eyes lit up. I had never seen green eyes so magnificent. I wanted to fall into them. He didn't blink once; I felt mine open and close, open and close. I felt so shy but instead of looking away all I could do was blink. His eyes were so mesmerizing. I felt like I knew everything about him without even knowing his name. He seemed to be the sweet and romantic type. I believed in love at first sight because I am a hopeless romantic not because I had experienced it before, until I saw his eyes. I wonder how long he had been staring at me for when my eyes met his, he was already gazing at me. I knew there was no turning back – this was it, he was it.

They were brown, but not like any other brown eye I had ever seen. I didn't want to look away. The sun hit them and suddenly they looked like gold. I had never seen anything so beautiful. She slowly blinked and each time she opened her eyes, I fell in love all over again. They were so mysterious yet I felt like she could read me just by her stare. I became numb just from looking at her eyes. I suddenly lost all touch that I had in my fingertips. Who knew eyes could do that to someone. I never believed in love at first sight until my eyes contacted hers. I knew there was no turning back- this was it, she was it.

.

XVII. What We Deserve

Many of the pains that us as humans encounter these days are self inflicted. We get burned by the fire but we were playing with it to begin with.

Same goes for love. We inflict self pain on ourselves when we ask for love from the wrong people. Really, if we ask for love in general. Love is the easy part, but if you find yourself asking for love, you're not in the right place.

No one should ever beg anyone to love them. When you beg for love, you might as well take your heart and throw it away. Everyone deserves to have the type of love that they give.

When we deal with people who don't love us the way we deserve, it's like making an appointment to break our own hearts.

If someone is not adding value to your life, it's okay to walk away and say goodbye. There are plenty of people out there waiting for someone like you.

Don't settle for anything less than what you truly deserve. When you encounter someone, who can't meet you half way, detach yourself from them. It's not fair for you to put in more work than them.

Do not play the waiting game. Anything that requires you to put off being loved, to question when they will come around, or wondering how long until their mind is made up, is a waste of your time. There are so many things about life and love that you can wonder about.

If the love starts to fade, it never was love to begin with because love never fades. If anything in the world is the closest to perfect its love. We as humans take love and turn it into something complicated. But love, it's the closest thing to perfect we have here on earth.

XVIII. My Question For You

What if I told you that you didn't have to hide anymore? Behind the scars and behind the tears. And that you can tell me everything you've been holding inside. Not only can you tell me but you can trust me. What if I asked you what you see when you look at your reflection? Would your answer be the same as mine? For you are far more amazing than what meets the eye.

What if I asked you to show me the real you? Would you run and hide because your insecurities break you down? Or will you take my hand and begin your story? I don't care where you've been or what you've done, I care about you.

If I told you how handsome and amazing you are, would you believe me? Or would you look down at your feet and question my feelings for you? What if I told you every night how much you mean to me? Would you be able to close your eyes at night without asking if it's true?

What if I told you I was by your side through thick and thin? What if I told you that our footsteps will never travel the past, but only the future? If I told you to trust me and that I wouldn't hurt you, would you believe me?

What if I told you, you'd never have to worry again? That if I wake up every morning and see your eyes, I will always kiss them goodnight. What if I told you, you had something beautiful inside? That God made you just for me.

And what if I told you that if it's not your eyes I get to look at I'd rather be blind? If I told you your laughter warms my chills, would you laugh a million forever's?

If you couldn't get enough strength to make it through the rest of the day, would you believe I'd be the 90% to your 10? If I told you that I see you, would you believe it's not the version you show off to the world? What if I told you I wanted to be apart of your life? Would you open the doors and let me in?

As 3:00 am approaches and you remember all the times you would lie awake feeling lonely- would you believe that 3:00 am next to me would bring you happiness?

Just tell me one thing; would you believe all those things?

XIX. She Was Everything

She was the stars, but you always wore your shades. You never did see just how bright she would shine. And she was the ocean, more like the waves, but you never did go near the water; you never did feel just how strong she was. She was the piece of art everyone wanted to have, but your eyes were never on her.

She was the moon, but you only came out during the day. She was summer, warm, bright and spontaneous, but you paid too much attention to the cold heart that sat in your chest.

She was the forest, and every tree made up who she was, but you cut them down to make something only you could use. She was a lighthouse, there to be your protection, but you decided to go some place else for help.

She was a storm, the girl that could sweep you off your feet, but you were the tornado and blew her away. She was fire, the fire that lit your cigarette, but you smoked her down to black ashes.

She was a heart, but unfortunately you wouldn't let her be yours. Your heart pumped blood throughout your body when angered but slowed down when it came to loving her and she deserved so much more than that.

XX.   Double Entendre

      Open windows, shut with a burst of air,
He said his heart was close but she wondered where.
      The wooden floors, with nails sticking out,
He said come closer yet she wondered about.
      The wallpaper, started to unravel,
He always kept her near, but she wanted to travel.
      The house was always dark, never was there light,
She could never stay too far, but she tried with all her might.

      The shutters were barely hanging on, against the house they'd knock,
She was in-between hard spots, like a brick and a rock.
      The door, although worn, stood tall and painted red,
Never again in love she'd fall, well at least that's what she said.
      The house was small, but the rooms were grand,
She hated being alone, but alone she had to stand.

      And on the rainy days, the house would tend to leak,
She never had freedom, so freedom she tried to seek.

      The bedroom was the darkest for the love had gone away,
She wanted to feel whole again but they feeling would never stay.
      The kitchen had no food; the cabinets were bare,
He knew she was unhappy the way her eyes would stare.
      The family room had everything but no family to gather,
She wanted to express everything but to him it wouldn't matter.
      There were no pictures on the walls, no love to spread around,
There was much that needed to be said but she never made a sound.

That house was old but there was always worse,
She wondered daily if her life was but a curse.
　　Some days it remained quiet, other days' quietness evolved,
They denied problems existed, but they needed to be resolved.
　　This house wasn't built to last when it stormed,
It was a rocky relationship because love barely formed.
　　When the sun is out, no sun shines through,
His heart is cold and she wonders what to do.

　　But when it's all said and done, that house… will never be a home,
And she knows that if she's trapped… she's never free to roam.

XXI.   I'm Not Hard To Love

    I used to want you back, and would have done anything to get you back in my arms. I used to wake up in the middle of the night, reaching out my arms to feel you. I used to think I was incomplete without you, that if you weren't mine, I didn't want anyone else. It was you I wanted, my eyes never wandered. I once heard someone say they were homesick, but for a person. I never knew what that felt like until you left.

    After you, new people came into my life, showed me different things but there you were still lingering on. I didn't want them, I wanted you. I told myself that I would get you back, no matter what I had to do.

    Oh, but how I was mistaken. How I fooled myself. It would never work. You don't walk away from the people who are important to you. And if you cared, you would have stayed.

    I used to make excuses for you. "It wasn't him, it was me", "he just needs time to find himself" but there is no valid excuse for when someone leaves us. I wanted to go back to you because I missed you so much, but there are so many other people out there that will treat me better and appreciate who I am as a person.

    Then it dawned on me, you didn't see my worth. Towards the end I felt like I was begging for your attention. Was that too much to ask? And I may not know many things but I know one thing for sure... With or without you, the world keeps moving. I considered myself damaged when you left. Suddenly the only questions in my head were, "why wasn't I good enough?" "what could I have done to make you stay?" Any person who makes you question yourself or your worth isn't the one.

But someone is going to meet me and be blown away. Someone is going to come into my life and give me back the love that I gave away to you. Someone somewhere is going to show me that heartbreaks are a thing of the past. Someone… somewhere is going to make me realize that I wasted too much time being hung up on you. And although it's natural to miss someone who was a big part of your life, there is someone out there who can do that and so much more. You had your chance and you threw it away. You should have held on to me because it's rare to find someone with a mind just as beautiful as their face. But someone out there will show me that I am not hard to love.

XXII. My Definition Of Love

     A lot of people have LOVE very confused.
Relationship goals, selfies together, and matching clothes.
And while those things are cute and nice, LOVE is much deeper than those things.

     Love is the butterflies in your stomach when your eyes meet, and the butterflies in your stomach when they are far away.
Love is carrying the pain of your partner because someway somehow you two have become connected.
It is the laughter shared between jokes and stories that only you two understand.

     Love is the inability to sleep at night because reality is finally better than your dreams; it's the inability to sleep when they are gone because their body isn't next to yours.
Love is asking how they are just because; it's asking how they are because you know something is wrong.
It is remembering their likes and dislikes, and picking out the perfect birthday gift.

     Love is many things, including waking up before the alarm goes off just to spend more time hugging them.
Love is running late for work because each time you give them a kiss you say "okay, just one more".
It is trusting them with your heart, knowing deep inside that they won't break it.

     Love is all the little things too. Making sure they ate, that they have their seatbelt on, that they get enough sleep the night before their big presentation.
Love is being equal; one does not do more than the other.
It is even caring for their feelings and watching your words in the dreaded disagreements.

Love is going to every grocery store in town for double fudge peanut butter icing because every store you've been to has ran out.
Love is also putting the last piece of cake back where you found it because you know as soon as they come home that's the first thing they will grab.
It is knowing that you only like 3 sugar cubes in your coffee and nothing more nothing less.

Love is the ability to be best friends, partners, and team members all in one.
Love is being able to sit in silence just you two and feel nothing but complete peace.
It is looking at the stars and comparing their eyes to the glitter that sparkles high in the sky.

Love is knowing that as long as you have them by your side and everything went wrong they are the one thing you have right.
Love is doing everything you dislike because it's everything they love.
It is through thick and think, up and down, forever and always.

XXIII. Find Your Person

Be with someone who makes you happy. And I'm not talking about the laugh here and a smile there. I am talking about being with someone who makes you really happy. The kind of happy you experience when you look over and admire their face… knowing they have no idea and all you can do is smile.

You must have someone who protects you. I mean really protects you. Not just keeping you out of harms way but protects what's beating in your chest too.

Be with someone who challenges you, someone who challenges you to see yourself in ways you never knew you could. Someone who believes in you and pushes you to follow your dreams.

You must be with someone who values you, not for what you can do or what you have but for who you are. Someone who see's everything about you and still accepts every piece.

Be with someone who see's right through you, the parts that you hide, the parts that you don't love about yourself.

You must have someone who has good intentions. Someone who isn't in it for what they can gain but in it because they know where their heart belongs.

Be with someone who lights up your world. And not just bringing rays of sunshine but being the sun.

You must find your person; don't conform to the heartless wonders of the world. Be full of life and laughter and then find your person to experience it with.

XXIV. If You're Anything Like Me

If you're anything like me, you carry an imaginary net and catch the stars late at night.

If you are anything like me, you do good to those who treat you well, but you also do good to those who treat you bad. If you are anything like me, your kindness gets taken for granted.

People like me have a hard time fitting in, mainly because we are made to stand out. Only thing is, I hate when the spotlight is on me. If you are anything like me, you've learned the language of the stars. On your lonely nights, they've been the only ones there.

If you are anything like me, you've learned the universal language, love. But no one understands a word you're saying because no one seems to speak it these days.

People like me don't see bodies we see souls and feel connections. That's because we've been put down because of our appearances too. If you're anything like me, being kind is your virtue and good luck to anyone who tries to make you cold. If you are anything like me, your mind often wonders to another place while your body is still here on earth.

If you're anything like me, your therapist is music and your therapy is a long car ride. You don't need someone to tell you how to handle your feelings- although words from a friend can be a cure to our self diagnosis.

If you're anything like me, you're the peace that people need. When their storms seem to never end, you become the rainbow that shows up in the sky.

People like me become rest to the restless. We invite them to escape the chaos of their world even though we to get lost ourselves- I think we tend to find our way by helping others find theirs. If you're anything like me, you are calm and balanced, sympathetic, truthful, and open hearted.

People like me, we're day dreamers, and night thinkers, with strong imaginations.

XXV. It's The Risk I Fear

It's not falling in love that I fear, it's waking up one morning not knowing that today might be the day they stop loving me. I'm not afraid to start holding hands with someone new; I fear that one day they'll decide to let go and leave me hanging. I don't fear getting close, getting to know someone all over again, it's knowing them so well that when they start to act different, that's what I fear. Like knowing when they are about to break my heart. It's not sleeping next to someone that I fear, it's how cold my body will feel when that person is gone, is what scares me.

I don't fear investing my time into someone; I fear giving up my time for them to only tell me it was all a waste. And I don't fear getting attached, that's a part of falling in love with someone; I fear, that one day, if they pull away they'll take a piece of me too that I can't recover. I don't fear love, or falling in love, I just can't shake the fact that maybe love fears me. Is it love that's avoiding me?

I don't fear giving my heart away, I'm more than willing; I fear that someday someone will take my heart and run with it, for it to never be found again. It's not putting my trust in someone's hands that scares me, it's the fear that one day they might lose grip and lose all the trust I had.

It's the risk of falling in love that I fear the most. There will always be a risk when it comes to falling in love but the greatest risk of all is not allowing yourself to jump. I have learned, the risk that scares us the most, ends up being most worth it.

XXVI. I Will Listen To Your Heart

When the tears fall down your face, I won't watch them fall, I'll stop them with a kiss.

And when your eyes are filling with tears and you're afraid to blink- look into mine; I'll hold your face gently.

Ill dry your eyes if you lay your head on my chest; I'll show you pain is not weakness as the tears flow from my eyes too.

You will never be alone, although you may feel like that at times. I hope in the back of your mind you think of me and know I will give you rest.

I want you to know, there is nothing wrong when tears fall down our face; I know there is a story being told that you're afraid to speak.

I'd listen to your heart, for that's where the tears start to form. It's our bodies way of telling us, that our hearts are upset.

It's easy to wipe tears from the eyes; I just hope I can learn one day to wipe pain from the heart.

And when you begin to speak, I'll hear it, the sound of sadness, and it will break me. It's the sound I hate to hear, when you're trying to be so strong but at any minute the waterworks will come pouring down.

I know how it feels, to just stand there as right in front of you your whole world is falling apart. There is nothing you can do but let the tears fall down your face. If that ever happens to you, will you come for me? Will you let me be the person who puts your world back together again?

XXVII. An Explanation Of Myself

Some nights I'll be quiet and won't have much to say. When that happens, I don't want you to think you did anything wrong. There will be days when I feel like crying because nothing is going right, but never forget you are the one thing I have right.

There will be times when I am looking you straight in the eyes and hear nothing you say. I'm not ignoring you, I promise. I'm just thinking about how lucky I am to have you. Some nights I'll lay in bed and feel alone, but don't worry I will know that I am not.

I don't know how to explain the way I am sometimes; I just need you to know that whatever I am going through you are not to blame.

Some days I don't feel like smiling even though you try your best to get me to do so. Just know that some things are going through my mind, and tomorrow will be better. There will be moments when I make a mess, and I apologize for not being perfect like you deserve.

I have a troubled soul sometimes, but I want you to know that you bring out the best of me.

There are times when I am a little rough around the edges, and I promise I don't mean to but you're the person I want to hold on to. Some days I will be distracted from all the good things in my life, but you will always be the one I reach for.

I may not be the easiest girl to put up with and sometimes I'll wonder what you see in me but I can promise I am worth it because I fight for what I love.

But regardless of all those flaws I have- you will be the one to pull me from my troubled mind and remind me where I am and what I have.

XXVIII.　He's My Paradise

If you asked me what Paradise meant- I would have told you going to the beach, or laying in the sand, feeling the sun on my face, listening to the ocean escaping the seashells, or looking up at a waterfall.

I would have told you Paradise is somewhere beautiful and unimaginable. Something you'd only see in your dreams. Paradise is perfect- too perfect for me.

If you ask me now what Paradise means, I'll tell you that it's looking into his eyes. It's waking up and seeing his face there.

Paradise is holding hands with him and staying close to his side.

That's paradise to me. Suddenly the beach seams mediocre, and laying in the sand doesn't compare to laying next to him.

Feeling the sun on my face doesn't feel quite as nice as feeling his hands. And listening to the ocean escape the seashells is beautiful until I hear his voice talking to me.

Suddenly I don't want to sleep, because he's better than any dream I've ever had. He's perfect- too perfect for me.

And that waterfall, I love to watch the water fall. But here I am, I am the one falling.

XXIX. First Free Flow

      Can somebody please tell me when I love you's and I miss you's became replaced with love you too and miss you too. Where did the I go? Straight to our iPhones and iPads maybe? Suddenly it's not about we anymore, there is no us. Hence why we've lost trust because we've lost us. It's all about the I. The I can do bad all by myself I. Why do you want to be by yourself? Alone, no communication so you change the radio station to find the missing words to your Facebook post. There is no I in team but there is me with letters moved around. We move we move, and we never stop moving. We stopped making time for those around us. Time, there goes the I in time. Time for me myself and I. Society has turned conversation into short word abbreviation and suddenly the human race forgot their own language. Nobody believes in love at first sight because suddenly our eyes become blinded by our screen light. Green light you can go, but now your head is down at your phone and angry drivers start honking their horn. Watch out don't hit that person, walking across the street looking down at their phone. Hello your friends ask, did you hear what I said? Dead, your phone is dying while your friends are dying to talk to you face to face. Our words have become limited because 120 characters force us to delete space to make room to fit in to click with someone else but we click through our likes instead. Click here to proceed with your payment, congratulations you will no longer feel lonely. Meanwhile the love your life is clicking to power down because she feels powerless because the energy to charge your phone takes the energy from her heart. Start stop pause play- you're watching videos on YouTube but you're getting interrupted by conversation around you. Apology?? not accepted, how dare they interrupt your time with technology. Do you get excited when your world lights up? No not the world you live in the but world that lets you know someone liked your selfie. Self which is positive during expression but self has became shut off from those around- round like the world accept your world stopped rotating.

Titled from its axis, you're off balanced and to become centered again you reach for your touchscreen. But I must check the weather, you say to justify. And that's fine until you contemplate whether to socialize personally or realize you'd rather do it virtually.

XXX. Poetic Rose

      Her body was on silk sheets, and every curve was protected by the softness of his skin right next to her. She would inhale and he would sigh. She was open and he could see right in. His fingertips were like honey dew and they would pluck her nectar that tasted so sweet. She used to hide, beneath the sheets but now the silk hides beneath her for he has made her feel like a beautiful queen. The tip of his nose ran along her body. He'd start at her head and end at her feet. But everywhere between those two locations received the love she deserved.

      Before him, she would cry herself to sleep sometimes, and wake up with a tear soaked pillow. He took that wetness and made her a pond, but the pond came from her after he had caressed her heart to no return. She realized then and there that those days of being half loved were over for he had caught her soul and released all he had to make her feel complete. There were marks on her body. Battle wounds she called them. Anyone before him tried to say that they were beautiful but she knew he was the only one who meant the words he said. He was the only one to touch them and not become afraid. He healed her battle wounds and filled them with her favorite flower, the rose.

      She likes to write, poetry to be exact, so he calls her the poetic rose. He took one look at her book and knew he needed to read more. He dug deeper and deeper and her hands became tied to his neck. The deeper he went into her mind the deeper he went into her body- it was then he could touch her soul and make her feel loved and wanted.

XXXI. What is.. Father?

He walked out and to my knowledge I would never see him again – but I did. Except it wasn't how I wanted too. I thought he was dying. He was fragile and so small his skeleton was piercing through his skin.

It was my father.

Except I don't feel right saying father – he was anything but that.

He was supposed to love me, protect me, and teach me. But he did none of that.

But here I am visiting him while he lays in his hospital bed – asking for forgiveness. And I did. I thought- its never too late, he's making his amends; he loves me. This is our fresh start. Right?

He received his transplant and vanished. Once again my heart was filled with unsaid I love you' s and broken promises. So, I thought – this is it I'll never see him again – but I did. Except is wasn't how I wanted too. He was in his brand-new car with a young Barbie with colorful hair in the passenger seat. I thought to myself – so this is all that matters to you? You spoke to me, told me you missed me but they were lies. Because as soon as you drove off I knew I'd never see you again.

Except I did but not the way I wanted too. Because this time you didn't even see me. Your eyes were on something else well someone else. But they weren't on your daughter who is all grown up now – who made it to her 20's without your guidance.

Hey dad did you know that I graduated college? And with high honors? Do you know who came to see me? Not you. Do you know I'm a writer? That poetry is my passion? Probably not because you don't even remember me on my birthday. I was supposed to be your blessing, my brother and I. Do you know my favorite color is teal? That I like to wear flowers in my hair? You don't know anything about me dad- please give me an explanation.

      I just wanted to feel loved by you. I wanted to feel wanted. I wanted to be your forever little girl. I wanted to wake up in the mornings and see you cooking me breakfast. I wanted to leave school to see you there waiting for me. I wanted to bring my friends home to meet my mom AND dad. I wanted you to pick me up when I fell, I wanted you to heal my broken heart, I wanted to hear you were proud of me, I wanted you to hug me, I wanted to hear you loved me. I wanted you.

      Throughout the years I taught myself to live without you- though that's the last thing I wanted. Throughout the years I spoke words to myself, "You're better without him, you're stronger without him". At first those words sounded nice but after some time I started to believe them true because... I AM, I AM stronger without you.

      You let my brother and I go- you had grasp of our little hands but lost the only grip you had. You let us fall. But we weren't down for long. Our mother picked us up and gave us all the love our little hearts needed to grow.

      My heart won't wait forever for you've crushed it enough. Now when I see you, you show me off like I'm some prize. Look how beautiful my daughter is and isn't she the most beautiful girl in the world? I grin but what you don't know is every time you say those things it rips my heart into little pieces, for all the times you never said those things while I was growing up.

XXXII. Lost In A World

Lost in a world of
ruin and misleading
People on their knee's
always pleading
Asking for forgiveness
for all their sins
Praying for happiness
and that hope always wins
Looking up at the sky
hands in the air
Wondering why the world
is so unfair
It is easy to say hello
but hard to say goodbye
You can say you are fine
but…that would be a lie
Torn apart in so many ways
wondering if this
might be the worst of your days
This world
is not as round as it seems
Not every star in the sky
shines and gleams
A blissful Sunday could end in rain
a smile could turn
with a touch of pain
The ground you walk
a hill to climb
The most perfect moments
frozen in time
Salty tears fall from the face
you start off strong
but lose the race.
The clock could stop
during the worst part
A perfect heart could rip apart

Lost in a world that
does not spin
Fighting a battle
you will never win
Making wishes on a shooting star
but never will it come
its too far
Want a place
you can call home
But you walk the abrasive path
all alone
Lost in a world where
the grass is brown
Where the bright smiles
turn to frown
On your knee's
touching the ground
Looking for a life
to be found.

XXXIII.   Unspoken Silence

There is a special soul in each of us
Some just... in touch more than others
That deep connection with the universe
And the world

The energy each soul gives off
Illuminates into another soul
Connections of energy portray through bodies
They latch.

Like a thunderstorm
When the power goes out.
Suddenly you become one with the darkness
It surrounds you
It becomes you

Sounds of silence
At first
It doesn't make sense
But even silence
Has a sound

Your ears hear your soul
Your heartbeat
Their heartbeat
The energy
Let it be what you hear- let it calm

The soul
Beautiful
Crying out -- unspoken
Silence has a noise too

If you cannot hear their unspoken words-
Your soul is too loud
Thinks aloud... instead of within

Just like rain showers
And rumbling thunder
Dark clouds
Your soul surrenders
The pain is gone

Thunder of release
Trapped under the floorboards
Lost and found
Rip it up
Search and find

The soul is enclosed- underneath the wound
It's sealed
Release the stream of the unknown

Freedom

Do you wonder your feelings of tomorrow?
Or anticipate your thoughts of
Today?

Wonder

Sit in the dark and release your monsters
But fear not-
It's just you
Looking into the mirror

Reflection.

XXXIV. Judged

People everyday – judged endlessly
By who they are
By who they want to be

Living life scared – troubled in fear
Wanting to speak out
But no one will hear

Why is race and color- such a problem?
Problems of the present
But no one will solve them

They say- don't judge a book by its cover
Yet everyday, some are judged by their color

They reach out a hand- to get turned down
And their proud smiles
Turn to frown

If they could look on the inside- and not the out
They would see a person like me
And what I'm all about

The sun is bright – and so is my mind
Look past the color, that's what you'll find

People today – they love to HATE
Especially when the opposite race
Is your soulmate

Trapped and alone- are the feelings of others
Hands to the sky for all our brothers
who died for their race –
When looking for freedom
Was their main chase.

I was taught to look past others greed-
To follow my dreams
And to succeed.

Color is something my eyes don't see- if all eyes were like mine- a happy world it would be.

XXXV.   The Stolen Heart

      Captured. Like loves first sight. Only that sight was nearly blinding. Stolen from me, the only thing I fear to get back. That is the heart. See, before it would beat. Now, I couldn't even tell you what it does. Searching. Like an explorer on the seas. And your eyes. Lost in translation even though I… know all the words. You see the world. I knew I wasn't apart of your world for when I looked into your eyes I did not see my reflection. Yet, I still admired.

XXXVI.   The Sunset In My Eyes

    When I wanted you to look at the stars, you told me you couldn't. For it made you feel small. I looked at you with a saddened heart. That was the last thing I thought about when I looked at the stars. I even smiled at the ones I couldn't see because I knew they were still there. I didn't think about how small I felt next to them because I was too busy looking at how they made your eyes sparkle. I wanted to hear you saw the sparkle in mine too.
    I would paint my eyes with a soft subtle pink, a burnt orange, and a deep lavishing red. With hopes that at least you'd see the sunset in my eyes.

XXXVII.   Beautiful Soul

Beautiful soul,
I know you want to give everyone a chance,
A chance to prove that they have a heart of gold.
But not all people do.
And you will find people who appear to have a heart as gold as their appearance,
But deep down inside you will soon find out it is as black as midnight.

Beautiful soul,
You are genuine and you are kind,
You would do anything for anyone.
But not all people will do the same for you.
And you will find people who seem so kind and so genuine like you,
But they only want something in return, something to make themselves feel better.

Beautiful soul,
I know it's hard to stay true to yourself,
Constantly being around people who do anything to change you.
You will find some people that want your innocence.
Make a promise to yourself, that you will not change for anyone or any soul,
Promise yourself that you can still be good in a world filled with evil.

XXXVIII. Change in Confidence

I didn't question myself often, I was very confident. I knew my worth and I knew how to love myself. I could pick myself up after being down several times, and depression was something I knew nothing about, for I always wore a smile on my face.

That all changed after I met you.

What a sweet charming smile you had. That was your hook. Wasn't it?

Dates on top of dates, and flowers at my door. Messages at 4am and kisses at 4pm. That was the catch. Wasn't it?

Because before I could open my eyes from that 4pm kiss, I see you with another girl. And your eyes are bright. So bright.

You held me by the arms but you are holding her by the heart. So gentle.

I questioned myself, for the first time in my life. I felt so alone. I suddenly forgot my worth and looked at myself with disgust. I didn't know how to love myself; what a mess I was. And I tried to get up, but I felt the force of the world on top of my chest and I was pinned to the ground. And suddenly I became the definition of depression. That smile I wore of my face doesn't fit anymore. It's on her now and it seems like a perfect match.

XXXIX.   He Never Told Her

You are perfect
You are wanted
You always have my attention
You will never need for anything
My love for you is a broad as the horizon
My love for you surpasses infinity
You make me happy
I would jump across the moon just to touch your hand
I am a better person because of you
We can make it though anything
Your beauty was all I saw
Your heart is grand, and so is your smile
You're beautiful
You're smart
I never loved a woman as much as I love you
I will never give up on you
You have me until the end
I'm sorry I hurt you
I'm sorry I never told you how I felt
I'm sorry

XL. Two Sides To Every Story

Cera:

It hurt like hell when he walked away
I was convinced he didn't feel a thing.
I did everything I could
Gave everything I had
I still couldn't make him happy with me.
I don't know where he is now
Probably in the arms of another woman
I know my arms gave the best love any man could get
He thought differently
I would have died for him
If it meant him living
He didn't have an explanation for leaving
Other than there was someone else better for me out there
I didn't believe him, not one bit.
And I still don't because I still want him
Nothing hurts more than thinking you're everything to someone
To only find out you're nothing.

Ryan:

It hurt like hell when I walked away from her
I felt every pain possible
She was grand and extraordinary.
She did everything she could to make sure I was happy.
And it worked.
But I had to leave, I'm dying.
I broke her heart but I couldn't let her see me at my worst
She would have stayed if I told her the truth.
That's how much she loved me
There is someone else out there
That can give her all she wants
And I died just thinking about how it isn't me
Nothing hurts more than finding your soul mate

Only for the universe to snatch them away
But it was just snatching me away
She was and still is everything to me
I wish I could have told her

XLI.   Poetic Rose Addition

Poetic Rose:

I used to be closed off, so bundled and tight.
I didn't want to let anyone in.
For the fear of being left.

I would hold onto my thoughts.
And they would linger on my paper.
For I was afraid of my words being entered into one's ear.

I was a rose.
But I had not yet bloomed.
I kept my petals in, I kept my petals tight.

Until water hit my petals and dripped onto the ground, and up the stem it traveled.
My petals started to unravel.

Suddenly words were flowing.
From my paper into ears, I wasn't bundled and I wasn't so tight.

Each petal that unveiled, the truth was set free.

The paper was my water, it always fed me back to life.
It gave me the courage to be fearless.
And not to fear.

I could imagine changing lives, and touching souls.

I knew what I had to do.

I had to transform. Unravel.

No longer was I the rose, I was the poetic rose.

Thank you for reading my first book. I enjoyed writing this book because for the first time I wasn't afraid of what people would say or think. I am a firm believer in saying what you feel. Because I was a person that held everything in, I have so much more to write and it only gets better from here. I feel like this book is just stage 1 of my conversion into the person I aim to be. I hope that this book had a positive impact on you and I'd love to hear your stories!

Contact Anastasia Lindsey:

Email: analarosapoetica@gmail.com

www.ingramcontent.com/pod-product-compliance
Lightning Source LLC
Chambersburg PA
CBHW031609110426
42742CB00037B/1505